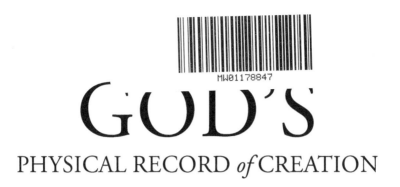

GOD'S
PHYSICAL RECORD *of* CREATION

RUFFIN RACKLEY

BA Geology, MS Geology

Trilogy Christian Publishers
A Wholly Owned Subsidary of Trinity Broadcasting Network
2442 Michelle Drive
Tustin, CA 92780

Cover design by: Cornerstone Creative Solutions

For information, address Trilogy Christian Publishing
Rights Department, 2442 Michelle Drive, Tustin, Ca 92780.
Trilogy Christian Publishing/TBN and colophon are trademarks of Trinity Broadcasting Network.

For information about special discounts for bulk purchases, please contact Trilogy Christian Publishing.

Manufactured in the United States of America

Trilogy Disclaimer: The views and content expressed in this book are those of the author and may not necessarily reflect the views and doctrine of Trilogy Christian Publishing or the Trinity Broadcasting Network.

10 9 8 7 6 5 4 3 2 1

Library of Congress Cataloging-in-Publication Data is available.

ISBN 978-1-63769-256-1 (Print Book)
ISBN 978-1-63769-257-8 (ebook)

To my daughter, Heidi Rackley, and to all the intelligent and educated people who come face-to-face with the question of what to believe concerning the creation of the universe.

ACKNOWLEDGEMENTS

Many sources of information gleaned from a multitude of sources over the past seventy years have contributed to the understanding of the subject of universe creation, and the author is very grateful to them all. The conclusions reached herein are those of the author.

A special acknowledgment is due to my very dear friend, Tina Colleen Marzec, for editing and correcting the manuscript. Not only has she done the yeoman work, but also she has encouraged me to finish this document and to make it as easily as possible to understand. Tina has been my guardian angel, and through her keen observation and action, she has given me three years of life and counting, by getting me medical attention when there were only two or three minutes to spare.

FOREWORD

by Tina Colleen Marzec

Founder, Biblical Heritage Preparatory School, Gr 1-12
Founder, Christian Independent Study Program,
K-12; Accredited by Association of Christian
Schools, International (ACSI), the Association
of Christian Teachers and Schools (ACTS), and
Northwest Association of Schools and Colleges
Education Consultant, High School
Principal, Teacher Gr 4-12
Author, *Christian Curricula Secondary School,
Parents' Guide to Homeschooling*

From a young age, I have been captivated by "back-in-the-day" stories told by my grandparents, especially when the topics were regarding names given to honor members of past generations, their preferences or interests, their customs and accomplishments, and how things have changed. This is history. It is through my grandparents' stories of their ancestors that I also developed a passion for researching and teaching genealogy. Scripture has modeled the importance of documenting history: of God's physical creation of the universe, of people and their heritage, and of their connection to God. God's recorded history provides documentation of the lineage of the Jewish Messiah, Jesus, as well as His promise that He will accept non-Jewish people as family members when they accept God as their Creator and the Lordship of Jesus and follow His teachings.

Learning and sharing that knowledge with others have been my obsessions since I was a young child. While in the third grade, I knew that I would be a teacher, and no one was able to persuade me into a different career path—not even the high school counselor who argued that I would be most successful in the medical field. She was totally wrong. "'For I know the plans I have for you,' declares the Lord, 'plans to prosper you and not to harm you, plans to give you hope and a future'" (Jeremiah 29:11. New International Version). God's plan was wonderful for me, and I am grateful that I heard His voice and followed His path.

My initial career in education began at a public junior high school (grades 7-9) as department chairperson and teacher of 250 students per day. The student population was a reflection of the middle-class neighborhood who valued education, peppered with a few gang members who had other goals in mind. I considered it an honor when one of the gang leaders told me to never feel afraid—that all of the leaders and their guys would protect me at any time, at any place.

This was a remarkable contrast to my last mission in a one-to-one environment, mentoring emotionally fragile high school students whose lives had been severely traumatized. Between these extremes, I navigated and thrived in the world of Christian education. By the end of this journey, I have been able to see how God's plan has guided me each step of the way, always building upon what I had learned in order to serve the next group of students and their parents.

During my career, I dedicated ten months of each academic year to teaching and developing curricula. During the two summer months, I enjoyed traveling to historic sites, visiting landmarks and geologic formations. The first, and most significant, was to Hawaii Island, Hawaii. To participate in the traditional luau was both a culinary and cultural experience that I could not have imagined, and being literally on the edge of a massive crater and viewing the 1974 eruption of the Kilauea volcano was the ultimate terrifying event! When our group began the tour from the parking area, the park ranger cautioned us about breathing the toxic sulfur dioxide gas and gave us damp cloths to cover our noses. While we were standing as close to the crater's edge as he thought was safe, he directed our attention to the depths of the massive pool of molten lava that was spewing red flares of matter into the air as the bright orange and black lava below continued to swirl feverishly. As I was experiencing this overwhelming power of nature, I noticed that a large edge of the crater on the opposite side suddenly separated and crashed into the bowl of molten lava. I motioned this to the ranger and asked if we were safe. His face told me the answer before he replied, "Let's get to our cars, NOW!" God's plan was not to harm me.

As I traveled throughout our country, I truly enjoyed many visits to the Grand Canyon National Park in Arizona and have been in awe of the layered bands of colorful rock, the depths of the canyon in contrast to the plateau, and the rushing cold waters of the Colorado River. I knew that God created it, but I have not delved into its history. I often camped in the rugged Anza Borrego Desert State Park, California, approximately one hundred miles east of the Pacific Ocean, and was interested in seeing the layered rocks of the canyon and the changes that recent earthquakes had made to their layers. Of course, I also enjoyed finding petrified rock, sea shells, and a few old items perhaps left behind by explorers or travelers through the ages.

Equally amazing is the opportunity now to reflect upon and to discuss with Mr. Rackley these and other experiences. I have always believed that God created everything, but I have not asked the questions "how?" or "why?" that Mr. Rackley has posed and answered.

During the process of editing his manuscript, Patience: *God at Work—God's Physical Record of Creation*, Mr. Rackley and I have had many in-depth discussions about his observations and conclusions, which he has thoroughly and patiently described for others to read, to ponder, and to apply to their lives. By reading his biography, I believe that it is apparent that throughout his lifetime, God has prepared him every step of the way to learn His secrets of the universe and to share them with others. This seems quite similar to Queen Esther, whose relative Mordecai said to her, "And who knows but that you have come to your royal position for such a time as this?" (Esther 4:14 New International Version).

Mr. Rackley has an incredible ability to clearly communicate complex issues in a respectful manner for those who are less informed than he. For example, I could relate his explanation of the significance of craters caused by meteorites to my Kilauea experience. By reading and discussing the details of his manuscript, I now not only have a greater understanding of geology, but also of God's love, compassion, and plans. Not coincidentally, this is Mr. Rackley's desire for all who read his written presentation of *Patience: God at Work—God's Physical Record of Creation.*

PATIENCE: GOD AT WORK[1]
OR
GOD'S PHYSICAL
RECORD OF CREATION

There is one point on which scientists and creationists agree: that there once was no universe even remotely comparable to the one in which we now live, but that it was created at a finite time and place. The scientific community has an obligation to search for the beginning of the physical universe, using all the tools they think will assist in that search. In the last forty to fifty years, considerable work has been done to advance that search and to answer some of the other mysteries still unresolved. New bodies of work have been advanced to address these problems; of these, the questions of the "primeval atom," dark matter, dark energy, and the nature of the Higgs boson are paramount. The Spirit will forever remain a mystery to scientific enquiry. Scientists have no way to deal with things that aren't related to atoms, nor can they explain the source of the power or energy needed to produce the universe.

Creationists believe that the earth and life on earth as it now exists was created a little over 8,000 years ago, but these views are not supported by observations and are not considered herein. The questions, then, are: what, and from what, and how was the universe created?

The "what" is the physical universe, which is so large that it is difficult to describe, and even the best-educated of today don't even try. Today's estimate is that there are 125 billion galaxies, each of which is composed of billions of stars. The location of our solar system in the Milky Way galaxy is in the constellation Orion's arm, which is 25,000 light years or approximately 148,000,000,000,000,000 miles from the center of the galaxy. Of course, everyone thinks in those terms—yeah, right! Then, think in terms of a society that has not yet developed a written language and its history of creation was verbally passed from one generation to the next generation many times, and yet the written version of Genesis is remarkably close to the physical record of creation which the Creator has left for scientists to read.

PATIENCE: QUARKS, SPIRIT, AND ATOMS

Creating quarks and atoms, then building a universe and a solar system with a planet suitable for human habitation, requires many steps, all taken in the proper order; and so it was in the creation of the physical and biological universe. It was not an event, but rather a process—a long, slow, exceedingly finely-orchestrated process.

Before considering how the universe was formed, it is important to have a good understanding of what was first created: the simplest atoms, from which all other things are composed—a single proton and an electron. The proton is a minute entity made up of three tiny bits of energy which are constantly spinning and orbiting each other. Two of these tiny bits of energy, called quarks, have negative charges and have the ability to switch to positive charges. The other quark has a constant positive charge equivalent to the other two quarks combined. These infinitesimal bits of energy have no mass—they do not weigh anything.

There is, however, another object in the proton called the "Higgs boson," which does have mass or weight. The Higgs boson was a latecomer to the subatomic scientists' observation and was given the nickname "God particle" because of the difficulty in finding it—and recently, the high energy required to prove its existence. A Scottish physicist, Peter Higgs, hypothesized that the space between the particles was filled by a heavy, sticky substance that provided the mass. Others describe it as an ethereal field or as an invisible vapor. Regardless of how it is described, it provides weight and acts as a rubber band that increases its force as it is extended. This holds the particles in close proximity in the core of the proton or neutron in opposition to their tendency to repel each other or just fly off. The nickname "God particle" may be much more important in the universe's creation and in its final destruction than presently perceived.

These God particles make up the nucleus of the proton, and with the addition of a negatively charged electron orbiting at an extreme distance from the others, a simple atom is formed: the element hydrogen, which has been assigned the atomic weight of (1) one. The space occupied by a proton is similar to the solar system in relation to their size, so they might well be called M (Mars), E (Earth), and V (Venus), and the Higgs boson acts as the center (sun) of the proton, with the electron like Pluto in our solar system.

The elements heavier than one are a combination of protons, either positively charged, and neutrons, a proton equivalent without charge. Stars and our sun burn hydrogen, and some of the lighter elements are produced in the fusion process, which also produces a great amount of energy. Hydrogen burning, and the associated processes that take place in the stars, are limited in their capacity to produce the heavier elements that produce heat and light for our entire solar system. In both the fusion and fission processes, tremendous energy is released by separating or combining the protons and neutrons, but no proton or neutron is destroyed; all that were ever created are still present somewhere in the universe.

The scientist, by definition, is unable to go beyond the physical universe and thus must define a physical, preexisting object from which to build the universe. The generally accepted object is possibly as small as an atomic nucleus, or perhaps slightly larger, called the "primeval atom." From this primeval atom with an incredibly high energy density, high temperature, and pressure, the universe was born. In a very small fraction of a second (1×10^{-36} or about two-trillionths of a trillionth of a trillionth of a second), this primeval atom went through cosmic inflation, which increased its size exponentially by a factor of at least 10 to the 26th power. This translates that an atomic nucleus would increase to one billion (1,000,000,000) kilometers or 621 million miles in diameter during that very small fraction of a second.[2]

There are at least two problems with this primeval atom and cosmic inflation. The first and foremost is the primeval atom. Was it always present, or was it a product of a previous universe collapse, or something else? The second problem is cosmic inflation and the postulated heat and pressure. The expansion factor of 10 to the 26th power should have produced the coldest place ever known, not the heat required for nucleogenesis; and without mass and confinement, why would there be pressure or heat? Undoubtedly, many other theories have been proposed for the presence of the nucleons and the initial temperature and pressure to initiate Big Bang Nucleosynthesis, but all from some pre-existing source with the same problem as the primeval atom.

PATIENCE: GOD CREATED THE UNIVERSE HIS WAY

The problem with the primeval atom is that it requires that the nucleons were created by some type of non-physical creator. There is a possible alternative to these views of the atom and its creation. The Creator, God, had nothing physical from which to create a physical universe and had no limitations, as the scientist does, regarding what could go into the makeup of the universe.

Something had to be created that could make the transition from God's realm into a new physical universe. The tiny bits of energy in the quarks and other subatomic particles were created in the space that the physical universe was to occupy. These newly created particles were performing no function without a system of organization. God directed bits of His Spirit into this chaos to bring that order. There was inflation, indeed—not cosmic inflation from an unknown source, but rather caused by God, our Creator. Upon the initiation of the Big Bang, the physical creation of the universe began! God inserted a tiny portion of His Spirit into every proton or neutron as it was being formed in the initial creation process. The protons and neutrons are indestructible, further identifying them as being created by God. They can be combined to form other elements in the fusion process, which occurs in supernova or star explosions, or they can deteriorate into daughter products, but they are not destroyed.

GOD SENDS HIS SPIRIT TO INITIATE THE BIG
BANG BEGINNING OF THE UNIVERSE

In the physical universe, the proton of the hydrogen atom is the initial building block for all creation. In addition to its role in the nucleus of the atom, the Spirit is the essential provider of mass or weight to enable gravity to hold the celestial bodies together in their orbits. It is basic to the order of the universe. This would suggest that the Creator created the physical universe and also holds creation together by the presence of His Spirit. In both the primeval atom case and the Creator-created case, the events following the first second are the same from that point forward, and the results agree with the observations.

PATIENCE: BIG BANG AND THE UNIVERSE BEGAN

It is irrelevant whether one prefers the "primeval atom" or the "Spirit insertion" into bits of energy; the events from the first small fraction of a second forward will be the same.

During the last fractions of that first second, new atomic nuclei formed until the end of the first second in a process called nucleogenesis. From one second through three minutes, the plasma (hot, ionized hydrogen) was under sufficient temperature and pressure that helium nuclei were formed in a process called Big Bang Nucleosynthesis. The expansion and cooling of the rapidly expanding plasma caused the fusion to cease at about the end of three minutes. Through continued expansion, the temperature of the plasma eventually declined and incipient protons and neutrons began to develop. Photons, which include visible light, x-rays, and heat, were also produced. From these subatomic particles only the simplest atom—hydrogen, made of one proton and one electron—was formed, sufficient for all the universe. All other atoms (elements) were created in various ways by combining these protons with neutrons.

The beginning was approximately 13.7 billion years ago, with an accuracy of 200 million years, more or less. With the formation of hydrogen, the Cosmic Microwave Background (CMB) was emitted, which has permitted the study, mapping, and dating of bodies and events in the universe. It raised the temperature of space to 2.7 degrees above absolute zero as it swept through space. Although cool enough that no light was emitted, the gas cloud, or nebula, continued to expand and began to separate into smaller clouds from which galaxies formed.[3,4]

Hydrogen burning is the primary process that goes on in the sun to produce heat and light. During the burning process in the core of the sun, the pressure and temperature are so high that the hydrogen nuclei lose their electrons. They are in such a highly excited state that the normally repulsive tendency is overpowered, and two protons fuse to form a deuterium nucleus. This is followed by fusion of the deuterium with another hydrogen nuclei to form helium^{-3}, then two helium^{-3} nuclei fuse into helium^{-4}, a stable element composed of two protons and two neutrons, thereby releasing two protons that are free to begin the process again. To produce heavier atoms, it was essential to create stars, which required the nebulas—dark clouds of gas—to begin forming masses from which galaxies and stars could be formed. The behavior of stars depends upon their mass; massive stars could reach the main stage of power and brightness in as little as 10,000 years and would also extinguish quickly. In as little as one million years, intermediate size stars, which includes the sun, could take as long as a million years to reach the main stage, where they will remain for up to twelve billion years. Smaller bodies formed from the early gas cloud will never reach the main stage.

PATIENCE: BIG BANG, THEN WHAT?

In the following chart, Time Line of the Universe, the events that have taken place in the progressive development of the universe and of the earth are compared to the 24 hours of a single day, to help the reader get the idea of the complexity of the creation process. The times referenced (xx) are lapsed time from the beginning (0) until today (23 hours, 59 minutes, and 59.99 seconds).

The original energy burst which created the physical universe and initiated time lasted about three minutes. As the rapidly expanding cloud of particles cooled, the light from creation dimmed and the universe became dark for about 380,000 years (2.5 seconds). All the particles had formed into atoms by that time, with hydrogen and helium being the principal atoms present. Even though it was cool enough that no light was emitted, the gas clouds continued to expand. As portions of these very large clouds began to rotate and flatten, small masses separated and became dense enough to form a star.

PATIENCE: GOD BEGAN TO BUILD THE UNIVERSE

The massive stars end their main stage with a supernova, which is a violent nuclear explosion that produces heavier elements. Continuing that process in a second and third generation of stars, each generation included billions of stars which could only produce elements based on the elements in the cloud in which each star was formed. This is the second phase in the process of building a solar system and the first generation of stars. These hot, bright stars quickly reached the main sequence phase, which consisted of fusing hydrogen into helium and other heavier elements. It is in this main sequence phase that heavier elements such as carbon, neon, oxygen, silicon, and iron were produced. When the iron core collapsed, it started a cataclysmic explosion—a supernova—which produced new elements such as calcium, lead, and uranium. Great quantities of new elements were thrown into space to rejoin the gas and dust clouds to be recycled into the next generation of stars, planets, and comets.

Since each generation enriched the gas and dust cloud with heavy atoms, there could be enough of the heavy atoms to produce the rocky planets that were required to achieve a completed solar system from that cloud. The work wasn't finished until after the earth was made into a hospitable place for life, including man; not too close to the sun nor too far away, turning on its axis at a reasonable rate, and having a tilt to its axis to provide the seasons.

Over about 100 million years (10.5 minutes), the original clouds of hydrogen and helium segregated into large, galaxy-sized clouds. Within these clouds, stars were also in the process of formation. There have been two generations of stars preceding the generation of the sun. There may be some of the smaller, first-generation stars remaining at this time, but the second- and third-generation are predominantly those still burning. The first-generation dominated the first 3.7 billion years (6 hours, 28 minutes), the second-generation dominated the next 4 billion years (13 hours, 28 minutes), and the third-generation dominated the past 6 billion years and will continue for a few billion years.[5]

Fortunately, scientists have been able to identify stars in all stages of formation, as well as in all stages of their decline and death, enabling them to generate a sequence that would look much like time-lapse pictures. There is no way to measure the time from the death of one star until the remains are incorporated into the next generation of stars; therefore, the lengths of these intergenerational periods are very uncertain. The third phase began after the death of second-generation stars with their increased, but still very small, proportion of the heavier atoms or elements.

TIME LINE OF THE UNIVERSE		
Billions of Years Ago	Time from Creation using 24-hour Clock	Event
13.7	00:00:00	Origination of physical universe—3 minutes' duration—Primary Event (nucleosynthesis)
13.6997 or 380,000	2.5 seconds	Light of initial burst of energy dimmed and universe became dark
13.600	10.5 minutes	Period of darkness in which gas clouds began to separate to form galaxies and stars
13.6 to 10.0	10.5 minutes to 6 hrs, 28 seconds	Very large gas clouds underwent secondary nucleosynthesis First generation of predominantly massive stars reached main stage, burned out, and exploded in supernova
10.0 to 6.0	6 hrs, 28 seconds to 13 hrs, 28 seconds	Second generation of stars formed from remains of previous stars and original gases
6.0 to 0	13 hrs, 28 seconds to today	Third generation of stars formed from remains of previous stars

From the immense nebula, or cloud of dust and gas, a portion perhaps several billion miles wide began to slowly spin. As it spun, it increased in density, and the denser region shrank, pulled together by its gravity. The speed of the rotation increased and eventually became a rapidly spinning disk. Due to the increasing density, the gas in the center of the disk became compressed, and the temperature increased. Then, when the core reached about 1,000,000 k and the pressure was high enough for nuclear fusion to begin, a new star was born. After the star, which was smaller than the first-generation stars but considerably larger than our sun, reached the main sequence phase, it may have remained in that phase for about five billion years before it began its decline to the supernova explosion. New, heavy elements[6] of dust, rocks, metals, ice, and minerals were thrown into the interstellar cloud of gas, which then became dark: "The earth was formless and empty" (Genesis 1:2 New International Version).

PATIENCE: GOD BUILT THE SOLAR SYSTEM AND EARTH

The fourth phase of building a suitable place for life began very much like the third. About 5.5 billion years ago, within an immense cloud that was many billion miles wide, a region within it began to slowly spin. As the spin increased, the region began to grow by accumulating more matter, which increased its gravitational pull. As the spinning continued to increase in speed, a disk began to form and attract more matter; rings formed in the disk, and the overall size of the disk was about six billion miles across. After a few hundred million years, the disc separated into a central core that became the sun. The rings developed clumps, which spun and eventually became planets and moons, all in approximately the same plane and orbiting in the same direction. The solar system continued to grow as it worked its way out of the nebula and began its orbit around the galaxy. The sun reached critical mass and began its life about 4.6 billion years ago. This new sun, a third-generation star,[7&8] began to produce heat and light (15 hours, 56 minutes): "Let there be light" (Genesis 1:3 New International Version) (day one); the earth was approaching its present size. The earth was initially a mass of cold fragments but eventually became a hot, molten mass caused by the heat of the impact of rapidly accumulating matter being added as chunks of all sizes fell to the earth's surface. One of these chunks was captured by the earth's gravity, but instead of falling to the earth it went into orbit around the earth as earth's moon (Genesis 1:16–18).

(See the timeline below, which lists the historical events as they occurred billions of years ago, references the Genesis account of creation, and a compares the time to a 24-hour clock.)

PATIENCE: GOD PREPARED THE EARTH FOR LIFE

When the surface of the earth cooled enough, thin plates of solid crust formed over the circulating molten interior. These plates were relatively thin, and the forceful movement of the molten interior caused the plates to touch, scrape, and bump into each other. In this process, some plates were pressed below others while others rose above others, forming highlands; however, the chief cause of highlands were the rims of impact craters caused by meteorites. These highlands were the site of early weathering and segregation of lighter elements from rock, as the earth cooled and water collected on the surface. The interaction of the plates, the weathering, and the erosion of the surface eventually produced continents of predominantly lighter rock, and the sea floor composed of predominantly heavier rock: the separation of the land from the sea (Genesis 1:9) (day two). The earth was turning on its axis daily to produce day and night, and orbiting the sun annually with its axis inclined to produce seasons (Genesis 1:4–5, 14–18) (day four) (17 hours).

During the first two billion years of the earth, the atmosphere was deficient in oxygen, but the thermal activity along the plate margins in the new oceans provided an ideal environment for the earliest life. The oceans were iron- and magnesium-rich, green in color, and oxygen deficient. Blue-green algae, a primitive form of single-celled organisms, appeared and flourished 3.6 to 3.4 billion years ago (17 hours, 51 minutes). By about 2.2 billion years ago, some of the carbon was fixed in dead organisms but not identifiable as fossils. The simple, single-celled algae did not have nuclei until about 2.1 billion years ago (20 hours, 18 minutes), but by about 1.8 billion years ago multi-celled algae appeared (20 hours, 50 minutes), and life in the oceans took on a much more diverse appearance. Along with the development of life in the oceans, the water became more oxygenated, and the color changed to blue. In some favorable conditions, massive deposits of iron oxide began to accumulate that would provide the world's population with iron.

From about one billion years ago (22 hours, 15 minutes) until about 560 million years ago (23 hours, 0 minutes), life in the sea continued a slow, steady change with the development of a variety of soft-bodied, multi-celled, worm-like animals, followed by other complex forms. These primitive life forms had little chance of preservation as fossils, and most of the rocks of that age have been metamorphosed to further diminish the record of that early life. With the deep burial of most of the un-metamorphosed rocks from this period, the fossil record is very sparse and difficult to find. The development of the primitive life forms demonstrates that God utilized an existing life to build a more complex life, just as the development of the stars and solar system was produced from the remains of previous stars. Not only are we made of God-produced atoms, each containing a small portion of God's Spirit, but we are all related to each other, and to all other life on the planet.

After the erosion of the iron- and magnesium-rich rocks of the early earth, earth processes began to produce enough lighter rocks to form continents which floated on top of heaver oceanic plates. These lighter plates scraped off and stayed on top of the oceanic plates as they subducted beneath them—the process that is now occurring on portions of the western North and South American continents. In some cases, enough of the lighter rocks were carried down to the subduction zone, where it melted and worked its way to the surface as igneous intrusions. These intrusions introduced new processes into the earth's crust as magmatic emanations and hydrothermal systems that produced several types of mineral deposits, sufficiently concentrated to be sources for modern commerce. On the surface of the continental plates at or near sea level, other processes began to operate to form limestone and dolomite, which became host to deposits of lead, zinc, and other minerals.

Calcareous shells and exoskeletons began to appear about 540 million years ago (23 hours, 3 minutes, 42 seconds), and for the next ten to thirty million years a great expansion in the diversity of life forms occurred. "Let the water teem with living creatures" (Genesis 1:20a–21 New International Version) (day five). At the end of this time, shell-bearing animals and trilobites were abundant. Trilobites were complex, mobile animals looking much like modern mealy bugs but with three lobes, many legs, and sizes up to fifteen inches long and eight inches wide. Many forms of life developed, became specialized, and then became extinct.[9] This abundance of buried lifeforms in the sea began the accumulation of organic-rich sediment that would later mature into petroleum. In the period around 350 million years ago (23 hours, 23 minutes, 45 seconds), primitive fish were living in the water, and as the ozone layer became sufficient to protect them from unfiltered sunlight, the first amphibians appeared, living on land and in the water. "God created the great creatures of the sea" (Genesis 1:21 New International Version) (day five). Land plants appeared about the same time. "Let the land produce vegetation" (Genesis 1:11 New International Version) (day three). The first plant to have seeds was a fern which appeared about 330 million years ago (23 hours, 30 minutes, 20 seconds). This may have been a prelude for the proliferation of land plants about 280 million years ago, which produced the first coal beds of the earth. Beginning about 120 million years ago, land plants made a major advancement with deciduous trees like the oak, elm, maple, poplar, and many flowering plants. These plants dominated the modern world. Grasses and grains also appeared, but the time since 60 million years ago (23 hours, 53 minutes, 42 seconds) has been of the flowering plants.

TIMELINE OF THE SOLAR SYSTEM AND EARTH			
Billion Years Ago	Genesis Day	Time from Creation, Using 24-hour Clock	Event
4.6	1 & 4	15 hours, 56 min.	The sun, a third-generation star, begins main stage, producing light
4.0	2 & 3	17 hours	Continents form on cooling earth surface
3.5	3	17 hours, 51 min.	Blue-green algae become abundant in sea
2.1	3	20 hours, 18 min.	Algae with nuclei add complexity to life
1.8	3	20 hours, 50 min.	Multi-celled algae develop
1.0	3	22 hours, 15 min.	Sea life becomes abundant and complex
0.56	3	23 hours	Sea life shows steady change and diversity
0.54	3	23 hours, 3 min. 42 seconds	Great expansion in diversity of life forms

0.35	5	23 hours, 23 min. 45 seconds	Fish and amphibians present, amphibians begin venturing onto the land, protected by ozone layer from unfiltered sunlight
0.33	3	23 hours, 30 min. 20 seconds	Ferns present— first seed-bearing plants
0.28	5	23 hours, 33 min. 45 seconds	Dinosaurs roam the earth
0.10	5	23 hours, 49 min. 30 seconds	Birds present
0.065	6	23 hours, 53 min. 42 seconds	Warm-blooded animals become dominant and dinosaurs become extinct
0.000,035	6	23 hours, 59 min. 59.23 seconds	Humans present
0.000,006	7	23 hours, 59 min. 59.96 seconds	Recorded history begins

0.000,002	7	23 hours, 59 min. 59.987 seconds	Time of Christ
0.00	7	24 hours	Today

The reptiles, of which the dinosaurs are major members, appeared about 250 million years ago (23 hours, 33 minutes, 45 seconds). While the dinosaur population declined about 65 million years ago, the reptiles as a class have survived. Mammals, the warm-blooded animals, appeared about the time the dinosaurs reached their peak. Mammals did not dominate among land animals until the dinosaurs' rapid decline began; in fact, the two events are probably related. The appearance of birds was about 100 million years ago (23 hours, 49 minutes, 30 seconds), and the modern mammals came even later. "Let birds fly above the earth" (Genesis 1:20 New International Version) (day five) and "Let the land produce living creatures" (Genesis 1:24 New International Version) (day six). The warm-blooded animals became dominant during the last 60 million years (23 hours, 53 minutes, 42 seconds).

PATIENCE: GOD HAS MAN TO WORK WITH

The physical record of humans and their relatives is very short in terms of the history of creation, mostly in the past 200,000 years; there is evidence that humans were present 3.5 million years ago (23 hours, 59 minutes, 42 seconds).[10] This evidence definitely indicates that they have been present on earth during the past 35,000 years or so (23 hours, 59 minutes, 59.23 seconds). Recorded history only began about 6,000 years ago (23 hours, 59 minutes, 59.96 seconds), and the time of Christ was 2,000 years ago (23 hours, 59 minutes, 59.987 seconds—thirteen thousandths of a second remained).

The culmination of creation is in the smallest increment of time. "Then God said, 'Let us make man in our image, in our likeness'" (Genesis 1:26 New International Version) (day six). From the creatures of the earth, God chose humans and called them Adam, or man (Genesis 1:27). Humans were not yet ready for the purpose God had for them, so He molded them into an acceptable form, and gave them a language and some social attributes. Then God gave them spirits, and "the eyes of both of them were opened" (Genesis 3:7 New International Version). God said, "The man has now become like one of us, knowing good and evil" (Genesis 3:22 New International Version). The spirit that God gave to man was, and is, a gift from God's realm: "And the spirit shall return unto God who gave it"; as each life ends, "Then shall the dust return to the earth as it was" (Ecclesiastes 12:7 King James Version).

PATIENCE: YOUR CHOICE

The decision to believe that the universe was created by the spontaneous, cosmic expansion of a primeval atomic nuclei of unknown origin, or to believe that the universe was created by a Creator with a purpose for the universe, goes far beyond intellectual consideration. The evidence that there was a plan and purpose for the universe is very well demonstrated by the careful progression of events from the beginning to the present. Only a creator, or God, could provide the substance from which the universe was made and the plan which is to be accomplished. God not only has a plan for the physical components of the universe, but He also has a plan for humanity, including you, on the earth, and He has the ability to ensure that it will be done.

It makes no difference whether you choose the creationist view of creation or not. Other than the creation of the earth, what do the creationists think about rest of the universe? Do they have any concept of the magnitude of the universe beyond the immediate vicinity of the earth? If not, they have a very limited concept of their God. Are the lights in a clear night sky decorations on a screen hung above the earth, or are they a very limited view of the vast space and the billions and billions of stars and galaxies that God has created? What things are impossible for God to accomplish? Perhaps to create the necessary genes to produce a baby in a girl; or for God's Son, Jesus, to lay down His physical life and reclaim it after three days in a tomb, then days later to leave the earth while many people watched? Nothing is impossible for God in this physical universe—not even to create the universe as it is just 6,000 years ago. However, the evidence in God's physical record would indicate that a much older universe is correct, rather than that which has been handed down over 3,000 years by memory from one generation to the next, until a written language was developed. The last eighty years have seen an explosion of knowledge, and much of that understanding has a bearing on things that relate to the creation of the universe. Why not adopt the attitude of my beloved grandpa, Rev. Jesse Louis Henderson, a circuit-riding Baptist pastor for almost eighty years: "Fit your faith to the facts"?[12]

PATIENCE: THE END? MAYBE!

The earth has about five billion years to go before the sun finishes its cycle into a dwarf. Of those billions of years, approximately two billion will likely be reasonably good for life in some form, but not necessarily for complex organisms such as humans. The sun will expand to encompass most of the four inner planets—Mercury, Venus, Earth, and Mars—before it goes into a supernova and scatters most of its mass into space, with only a small dwarf dull sun remaining. The remnants of the solar system probably will eventually join remnants of other stars in another nebula, from which a new generation of stars and solar systems will emerge. How many times the cycle can be repeated is probably limited by an ever-expanding universe and the decreasing density of the gases and debris in the nebulas, until it is not possible to create new stars many billions of years in the future. It is already 13,700,000,000 years old, more or less.

However, the Creator may have other plans and decide to end it. If the small portion of God's Spirit, or the "God particles," that were inserted into every proton or neutron at creation were withdrawn, the universe would become complete chaos; everything from the quarks to giant stars would lack anything to hold them together. The sun and all the other stars would cease to shine, as the heat and light already created would be dissipated. Likewise, all the planets, comets, and nebulas would disappear without a whisper.

PATIENCE: WHY?

The study of the creation of the universe and all of its complexities has been most interesting and challenging.

However, along with the interest, there is a lingering question that never has had an answer, and that is: Why? Why did God create this unbelievably large and complex universe? Why did God pick this earth out of the hundreds of millions of planets, some come and gone, that are or were suitable for life? Why did God create life on such a minute speck of dust as the earth on the outer fringe of the Milky Way galaxy? Why did God select a herdsman, Abraham, from a tribe of people wandering in the hills from the Mediterranean Sea eastward down the valleys of the Tigris and Euphrates to Persia? Their language was largely borrowed from the various tribes they encountered in their wandering, and they had no written language of their own for another 1,000 years or so after God appeared to Abraham and promised to build a nation of his descendants, the Hebrew people. These wandering tribes also encountered other religions as they moved about, and probably participated in some of them, so the concept of God was not entirely new to Abraham when God spoke to him and he humbly responded. However, this encounter between God and Abraham is the defining event separating the Hebrew religion from all the other religions, then and now.

Moses is credited with recording the oral history of the Hebrew people in Genesis and the four following books of the Old Testament. Moses was educated in Pharaoh's household, which almost certainly had an influence on him as he recorded the first twenty-seven verses of Genesis chapter one, in which he recorded creation. Even so, his understanding of creation was just a glimpse of the wonders that took place to produce the results that he saw. Except for an improvement in the science of astronomy, man's understanding of creation did not change for thousands of years, until about 1,500 AD, when knowledge began a transition through exploration of the earth and observations of natural events.

While this knowledge has not changed most churches' view of creation even today, it has not mattered to people attending those churches. A much more expansive view of creation has become possible over the past hundred years, but sadly, most of the earth's inhabitants are not even slightly aware of the information nor the magnitude and wonders of the earth's beauty. It is unfortunate that those who are aware of these changes may be offended by those who hold tightly to the traditional church view that approximately 6,000 years ago, over a span of six days, God created the universe and the earth as we now see it. For those who accept God's role in creation, there is no conflict between science and the Genesis creation account.

The answers to these questions are nowhere obvious, but there is a possible suggestion of "why" in the Gospel of Jesus Christ according to the apostle John. John uses *world* a number of times in context, suggesting the meaning of "total creation, the earth, or all-inclusive humanity." Jesus likewise uses *world* several times in His teaching at the Last Supper and immediately afterward. Perhaps a little stronger suggestion of the purpose for the world, this earth, is John 3:16 (New International Version), "For God so loved the world that he gave his one and only Son, that whoever believes in Him shall not perish but have eternal life." This great love is an amplification of the love expressed in the first commandment: Exodus 20:3–6 (New International Version). "You shall have no other gods before me…for I, the Lord your God, am a jealous God…showing love to…those who love me and keep my commandments." This love is defined in the treaty language of the ancient Near East as the "love" owed to a great king, and was a conventional term for total allegiance and implicit trust expressing itself in obedient service.[11] This is a two-way bond between God and His subjects or believers. Therefore, it appears that the purpose of creation is most likely to create a multitude of souls to serve God in some capacity in heaven. These souls will have already given their allegiance to Him while on earth.

As far as the believers are concerned, their opinion regarding the origination of creation is not important, because they have given their allegiance to God, but it is vital to those who are finding their way to their salvation and to their eternity. To those who have been exposed to some science theories before they are offered the chance to meet Jesus, it can make the difference between accepting or rejecting Jesus Christ as Lord—which is depressing.

When considering creation, is it possible that creation was without purpose or plan? Throughout the history of the universe and the earth, there are many instances of events happening for a purpose that produce a benefit for later use. The subject of the purpose and plan of creation evokes a certain sense of fatalism, but that is not necessarily the case, because freedom of choice may go down to the molecular level. It is distressing that in the modern and post-modern world, people in general have no concept of sin and believe that they have no need to be saved from its consequences.

Deciding to answer the call to accept Jesus as Lord of our life involves a choice for which there are three possible answers: 1) say YES and become a child of God and coheirs with Jesus, 2) say NO and reject the offer, and 3) DO NOTHING and hope that you don't die before you do make the choice. But what do the choices mean in one's life? First, it is important to realize that the birth of a child creates a soul that will last forever, first in the human body; after the body dies, the soul continues to exist in the presence of God in heaven, or the soul loses its connection with God and goes into Satan's hell below, separated from God and His followers forever.

Accepting Jesus as Lord has an immediate benefit, beginning with the peace it gives to the child of God, and will continue to provide benefits throughout the natural life. To go to heaven when the body dies is considered to be an extremely pleasant experience; and to serve God in whatever capacity may be offered is a privilege that will continue forever and forever.

To reject God and to say "no" to God's offer is to be forever disconnected from God, committing one's soul to everlasting loneliness, anguish, agony, pain, and despair. It is considered the unforgivable sin, because the decision cannot be reversed after a person dies. However, the loving God of creation desires to be connected to all people and will welcome each person into His family of believers, as He has all others, when a remorseful soul has admitted the mistake of rejecting God's gift and confesses that decision as a sin and asks for forgiveness. For those who reject God after being fed anti-god teaching, literature, or associations for a long time, there is probably no hope. But for those who have turned away from God after a bad experience in their church or other relationships, and have accepted an alternative in place of God such as the secular, godless Big Bang, there is much hope that they will feel compelled to return to God. As shown earlier in this document, the Big Bang is actually the beginning of the creation process and is just the first of a very large number of similar events needed to complete the present state of the universe.

For those of you who are choosing to "Do Nothing," you may take some comfort in knowing that a very large share of people, upon first hearing the gospel of Jesus Christ, His death on the cross, and His burial and resurrection on the third day, also choose to do nothing. Regardless of the many times you have heard the message and still do nothing, please realize that you are taking a risk of losing the opportunity by a sudden ending of your life. The grievous consequence is that you will definitely not participate in the peace and calm that accompanies a life lived as a child of God. While the gift of being a follower is free to you, it definitely had a price, which was paid by Jesus on the cross, and you must to do three things to acquire it: 1) you must confess your sins to God, 2) you must ask God for forgiveness, and 3) you need to profess your acceptance to others. This is commonly done in a church setting, but it is not required.

Sin is anything that separates us from God. In addition to the fact that we are separate from Him at the beginning, or birth, we absolutely must make the free choice to unite with Him through our acceptance of Jesus Christ as Lord. Most people would understand the separation from God as being unconnected—they need to get connected. However, to do this they need the right equipment, which is a contrite and humble heart. This free gift is not because you deserve it—for you will get what you deserve if you reject God's gift—but it is offered because God wants you.

Yes... YOU!

AFTERWORD

by Tina Colleen Marzec

The predicament now seems to be exactly how to place this life-changing message of God's creation into the hands of those who do not yet know Jesus, or who are uninterested. This book may be the key to unlock the door to their future with Jesus and a life connected to God and to other believers. Perhaps it is you, the reader, who may have been placed here "for such a time as this" (Esther 4:14b New International Version).

This subject may be controversial, which may spark conversations for you, the reader, to express your opinions and to offer Scripture references that either support or disprove Mr. Rackley's thesis. As a seasoned educator with experience in developing courses designed for each individual to understand the content, I pose a few suggestions for you to follow if you wish to assist others to have access to this God-inspired book.

1. Pray to God, asking how you can be of service to Him in sharing this message.
2. Provide copies of the book to your pastor, church leaders, family members, other loved ones, friends, and neighbors. Personalize each with a comment, Scripture, or words of encouragement. Sign your name.

3. Introduce yourself and Mr. Rackley's book to pastors and leaders of other congregations.
4. Encourage church leaders to create Bible study groups that will use the book as a basis for the study of God's creation. Add several copies to the church libraries.
5. Encourage Christian schools to add several copies to their libraries.
6. Request your local public library to include copies in the Christian and science sections.
7. Encourage Christian high schools to adopt the book as a textbook or supplemental resource material for their existing general or physical science courses.
8. Purchase or request that your church purchase air time on secular radio, internet sites, TV programs, etc. to promote the book.
9. Purchase or request that your church purchase air time on Christian radio, Christian internet sites, Christian TV programming, etc.
10. Request small, local bookstores to offer the book for sale.

"Call to me and I will answer you and tell you great
and unsearchable things you do not know."
Jeremiah 33:3 (New International Version)

REFERENCES CITED

1. Ottoson, Dick. (Rev. Richard). "Patience: God at Work." Sermon, September 10, 2006. Used with permission.
2. "Timeline of the Big Bang." Wikipedia, Wikimedia Foundation. Last modified 7 February, 2007.
   "Graphical Timeline of the Big Bang." Wikipedia, Wikimedia Foundation. Last modified 22 January, 2007.
   "Cosmic Inflation." Wikipedia, Wikimedia Foundation. Last modified 12 February, 2007.
   "Big Bang Nucleosynthesis." Wikipedia Foundation. Last modified 8 February, 2007.
   Wikipedia, the free encyclopedia, http://en.wikipedia.org/.
3. Overby, Dennis. "Scientists Say Map Proves Big Bang." *The New York Times in Seattle Post-Intelligencer*. February 12, 2003.
4. Lemonick, Michael D. "The End." *Time*. June 25, 2001, pp. 48–56.
5. Green, Paul J. "2001 Star." *World Book Multimedia Encyclopedia*.
6. Tierney, John. "Exploding Star." *Discover*. July 1987, pp. 46-6.
7. Recer, Paul. "New Planet Found in Distant Space." *Seattle Post-Intelligencer*, The Associated Press. July 11, 2003.

8. Cowen, Ron. "Galaxy Hunters, The Search for Cosmic Dawn." *National Geographic.* February 2003. Pages 2-29.
9. Moore, Raymond C. *Introduction to Historical Geology.* McGraw-Hill Book Co., Inc., 1949. 536 pages.
10. Lemonick and Dorfman, Andrea. "One Giant Step for Mankind." *Time.* July 23, 2001, pp 54-61.
11. New International Version Study Bible. Exodus 20:6.
12. Henderson, Rev. Jesse Louis (1844–1940), was a Confederate soldier throughout most of the Civil War. He had no formal education other than home schooling, and the experience gave him a love for learning and prepared him for life. After attending Mississippi College for a few months, he was ordained as a pastor at Pleasant Grove Baptist Church in Pontotoc County, Mississippi. He was Ruffin's maternal grandfather, a very wise and forward-looking man.

ABOUT THE AUTHOR

Ruffin I. Rackley
BA Geology, MS Geology

Ruffin was born November 14, 1925, into a three-generation household in Pontotoc County, Mississippi, where his maternal grandparents were reaching the age and physical condition to need some assistance. His grandfather was a Confederate soldier who later became a Baptist preacher, founding about a dozen small rural churches. This was a very comfortable environment for Ruffin and his three older brothers. They were taught the gospel of Jesus Christ from an early age; it was always there in many forms and conversations.

Both of Ruffin's parents had some college education. His maternal grandparents were gatekeepers for the two younger boys while parents performed their jobs. His father sold and installed generator-battery sets for rural homes; his mother and two other ladies established a school for the neighborhood children in a little one-room building the county owned next to the local church. The education opportunity improved for the local children over the next few years; Ruffin finished high school at the county seat.

Ruffin was drafted into the US Navy during the middle of his senior year on December 1943 and served over three years, principally in the San Francisco Port Directors crew, handling explosives shipments to the South Pacific. Ruffin began college at Mississippi Delta Teachers College where he was introduced to geology while enrolled in a geography class and decided to make geology his major. The teacher suggested that he go to the University of Tennessee for further study. He graduated with a BA after the summer quarter of 1950 and was awarded a master of science degree after the fall quarter of 1951.

It was in the geology class during the summer quarter of 1949 that he read the textbook account of geology history that the universe was much older than six thousand years, a concept that had been proposed by some Bible scholars. This discovery sparked Ruffin's curiosity that began a continuing lifelong study of the physical record of God's creation. During his discovery process, he systematically documented his observations, compared them to the knowledge available at the time, and he confirmed for himself that the origin of the universe is God. Ruffin was compelled to document his conclusions, a feat that he could not have accomplished until the knowledge was completed some forty to fifty years later.

During the last year at UT, Ruffin met a fellow Navy veteran, Martha Maas. They were married a year later on March 21, 1952, the day after Martha received her master of science in business education. Ruffin and Martha began their life together in Gate City, Virginia, just a few miles north of Kingsport, Tennessee. Martha taught business education courses at the local school while Ruffin began his work searching for lead and zinc in the Knox formation in one of the ridges in Virginia. Ruffin continued the search for mineral deposits at two other locations in Virginia and one in North Carolina until mid-June in 1957 when he answered the call to find uranium for national defense at Riverton, Wyoming.

Ruffin's work in Wyoming was much more productive, and after only six weeks, late July 1957, he led a crew into a new area where a major uranium deposit was found. This deposit contained twenty million pounds of uranium yellowcake. Exploration and development activity did not stop on that property for about forty-five years. A few years later in 1968, Ruffin and his crew found another deposit containing about ten million pounds of yellowcake in a geologically similar area of Wyoming.

During the sixties, a member of Ruffin's staff, Dr. Philip N. Shockey, made the important observation that the uranium mineralization occurred on the edges of oxidized sand bodies that had previously been organic-rich sediment. This led Ruffin to expand his research of bacteria in the leaching of copper mine wastepiles to the possible role bacteria may have played in the accumulation of uranium. He soon found that the same bacteria that aided in leaching copper were active in the development of uranium deposits, and another group of bacteria was active in the organic rich sediment. The two groups of bacteria working together produced an oxidation-reduction barrier that accumulated uranium and other elements.

The US Atomic Energy Commission learned of their work and requested that it be presented to their Annual Uranium Symposium in 1968. This work had not been committed to paper at that time, so it was divided between Dr. Shockey's idea of source beds and solution fronts, and Ruffin was left with figuring out how the concept actually worked. From this effort, *Concepts and Methods of Uranium Exploration* was developed and was presented to the AEC symposium and printed in the 1968 Wyoming Geological Association Annual Guidebook. The ideas were amplified and applied to the geology of the Gas Hills uranium mining area and published as *Environment of Wyoming Tertiary Uranium Deposits* and published in *Bulletin* of American Association of Petroleum Geologists. The ideas were further refined and published as *Origin of Western-States Type of Uranium Mineralization in Handbook of Strata-bound and Stratiform Ore Deposits,* edited by K. H. Wolf 1976, volume 7 chapter 3.

During the remainder of his career, Ruffin worked mostly in the Rocky Mountains. During these years, Ruffin and Martha lived in Salt Lake City area twice, returning to Riverton and Casper, Wyoming; Houston, Texas; and Denver, Colorado before seeking shelter from the high-altitude sun in Anacortes, Washington, in 1997.

After moving to Anacortes in 1997, Ruffin, relying on his parents' admonition to remember 2 Timothy 1:7 (KJV), "For God hath not given us the spirit of fear; but of power, and of love, and of a sound mind," started documenting his thoughts on God's physical records of the creation of the universe. At first, he titled his work *Patience: God at Work* and has later revised it to add, *God's Physical Record of Creation.*

Martha and Ruffin enjoyed retirement in Anacortes by being reunited with their adult children, creating new friends at church, and appreciating the lower altitudes and cloudy skies. Later in 2017, as the demands of living independently became burdensome, Ruffin and Martha moved into senior housing in the Seattle area. Martha passed away on October 17, 2019, after sixty-seven-and-a-half great years together.

CPSIA information can be obtained
at www.ICGtesting.com
Printed in the USA
LVHW041945061121
702610LV00005B/190